Self-Esteem

Enhance Your Self-Assurance, Ascertain Your Value, And Cultivate A Strong Sense Of Self-Worth Through The Application Of Hypnotherapy

(Cease Adopting A Victim Mentality And Enhance Your Self-Esteem)

Wilfred Chambers

TABLE OF CONTENT

Is There An Equivalence Between Self-Esteem And Self-Confidence?..1

Overcoming Shyness..7

Stop Negative Talking..14

Introversion, Shyness, And Love 23

Comprehensive Instructions For Enhancing Listening Skills..33

The Rationale For Establishing Objectives........39

Enhancing Self-Perception 45

Recognize And Address Concerns Regarding Your Self-Esteem 62

Negatives Thoughts..71

What Factors Contribute To The Erosion Of Our Self-Confidence?...91

Is There An Equivalence Between Self-Esteem And Self-Confidence?

Self-esteem and self-confidence are frequently employed synonymously. While there may be certain resemblances between the two concepts, each exhibits distinct attributes and qualities.

Self-esteem and Self-confidence defined

Psychologists commonly define self-esteem as an individual's assessment of their intrinsic worth or value. This attribute is frequently connected to the aspects of an individual's conduct, sentiments, convictions, and physical presentation. It is also commonly known as self-respect or self-worth by others.

In contrast, self-assurance is a demeanor that enables an individual to accurately and optimistically evaluate their own persona and capabilities. It exhibits a positive relationship with optimism, assertiveness, affection, independence, pride, emotional maturation, and adeptness in handling constructive criticism.

Self-esteem is grounded at a more fundamental level as it encompasses an individual's entire existence, whereas self-confidence pertains to either the entirety of a person or specific facets of their character. An individual who exhibits assurance in a particular matter may not necessarily possess a profound sense of self-worth. Let us consider the depicted personality traits commonly associated with individuals often portrayed as 'jocks' in cinematic portrayals. These individuals, commonly revered as sports heroes, are frequently portrayed as embodying the essence of confidence within their performance on the field. Regarding inter-personal relationships, individuals of this nature often partake in bullying behaviors and assert their self-worth upon others—a striking illustration of individuals characterized by diminished self-esteem. Similarly, individuals who are passionate about movies are often portrayed as possessing remarkable problem-solving abilities, yet lacking the confidence to articulate their process of solving complex mathematical equations.

In both instances, individuals who are academically-inclined and athletically-driven demonstrate a sense of self-assurance within their specialized domains; however, they exhibit a deficiency in the requisite mindset necessary to conduct themselves in a mature manner.

Men who possess confidence exhibit a precise evaluation of their abilities and possess an innate trust in the future that awaits them. They possess a satisfactory level of self-determination, which empowers them to pursue their objectives, aspirations, and ambitions. They possess a practical outlook on life and are capable of acknowledging the reality that circumstances may not always align with their preferences. They are aware of their limitations as much as they are cognizant of their potential. They have the ability to take a step back and evaluate their circumstances when things deviate from their original plans, viewing setbacks as chances for refinement.

This attitude facilitates their acceptance of the possibility that they may not achieve success in all endeavors or attain all desired outcomes. Henceforth, their aspiration to achieve greatness in their endeavors is moderated by their acknowledgement of the prospect of encountering failure.

Self-esteem enhances an individual's self-assurance, just as a deficiency thereof manifests in a person's level of confidence. The way in which one assesses their self-worth with respect to their professional undertakings, accomplishments, societal standing, and overall life goals displays a significant connection to their ability to exude self-assurance. Frequently, individuals of the male gender who possess a diminished sense of self-worth exhibit inadequate self-perception and contend with an inherent sense of inferiority. They do not perceive themselves as devoid of merit, inconsequential, insignificant, and devoid of affection.

In the event that you experience feelings of timidity or seclusion, it is imperative to ascertain whether these emotions stem from diminished self-worth or simply insufficient self-assurance to navigate social situations. In practical scenarios, this delineates the distinction between lacking knowledge regarding the appropriate course of action (confidence) and lacking belief in one's own abilities to accomplish the task (esteem).

Overcoming Shyness

Fortunately, one has the capacity to overcome their shyness and lead a fulfilling and purposeful existence. Occasionally, we may feel disinclined to engage in conversations with others due to apprehensions regarding their reaction towards us or our own subjective assessment of their compatibility with us. Are there any negative consequences associated with the realization that you do not establish a harmonious connection with another individual? Suppose you encounter an individual at the social gathering hosted by your closest companion, and after engaging in a brief conversation, it becomes evident that there are no shared interests or compatibility between you. It is highly improbable that a friendship could develop under such circumstances. That is acceptable. There were no negative consequences. It is not necessary for you to cultivate friendships with every individual.

Engaging in meaningful dialogue with individuals who hold similar viewpoints and convictions proves to be highly gratifying. Engaging in conversations with individuals who possess contrasting perspectives can also offer valuable insights and broaden one's understanding. Regrettably, when an individual is afflicted with reticence, it acts as a barrier that obstructs their ability to perceive and comprehend the myriad opportunities and experiences that the world presents.

Prior to discussing strategies for overcoming shyness, it is imperative to delve into its conceptualization and comprehend its ramifications on one's mental and physical well-being.

Timidity: exhibiting a proclivity to evade or distance oneself from something due to feelings of unease, apprehension, or antipathy.

Can you observe a recurring pattern in this context? Virtually all of the symptoms that individuals with low self-confidence exhibit can be attributed directly to a deficiency in self-esteem.

Shyness exhibits three core characteristics: Adverse Self-Evaluation - Social scenarios prompt heightened self-consciousness and attentiveness towards how one is perceived by others. One may experience a sense of inferiority, perceiving oneself as unworthy compared to others who possess beauty, intelligence, or talent, leading to feelings of being an outsider or intruder.

Preoccupied with Deficiencies - You are excessively preoccupied with conscientiously acknowledging and magnifying your perceived inadequacies, thus impeding your ability to recognize and appreciate your positive attributes.

Negative self-talk refers to a tendency to digress into a stream of thoughts where one highlights and emphasizes all the negative aspects of oneself. One commences with a seemingly mundane concern, such as the perceived dissonance between one's footwear and attire, but eventually proceeds to dismantle their entire appearance or conclude that they lack the aptitude or intellect to be in the presence of individuals perceived as more accomplished.

Shyness tends to resemble or evoke sentiments of anxiety. In the event that someone approaches you, you may experience difficulty articulating your thoughts due to anxiety, causing your speech to become incoherent and impairing your cognitive abilities. All of these physical symptoms further convince you of the above traits. Although you may find yourself rendered speechless, your mind is hyperactive, diligently highlighting every one of your embarrassing reactions as a direct result of the anxiety it is evoking.

Shyness encompasses more than just a weakened sense of self-worth. While it is likely that the condition initially manifests in such a manner, it is influenced by a variety of distinct factors. Throughout the years, you have been labeled as an individual with a reserved demeanor, and you have acknowledged and embraced your innate shyness. You have not made any effort to deviate from the established norms, as that label is one that you have embraced. This is impeding your progress.

Have you ever experienced a profound sense of self-satisfaction stemming from accomplishing something remarkable or acquiring a brand new ensemble that impeccably flatters your figure and exudes elegance? You are experiencing a sense of elation and confidently approach a social gathering with the intention of socializing, yet abruptly realize that you are afflicted with shyness. The feeling of confidence dissipates entirely, and you find yourself once again resigned to becoming a mere observer on the sidelines. Remove that label and assign yourself a fresh designation. Now is the opportune moment to engage in the practice of Positive Thinking. You are an individual with self-assurance who thoroughly enjoys engaging with unfamiliar individuals. Practice it repeatedly until you internalize it and persuade your mind that you are not a passive observer in social situations. You possess an extroverted nature and derive great pleasure from engaging with unfamiliar individuals.

Stop Negative Talking

The world is already immersed in an ample amount of negativity. If one's mindset is consistently negative, including one's internal dialogue, it sets a detrimental precedent for oneself. Do not entertain the notion that you are incapable of achieving something or lacking in value. Do not permit the dissemination of such pessimistic discourse to escalate. Individuals tend to magnify trivial circumstances, yet what truly occurs is their cognitive faculties meticulously analyzing situations and drawing exaggerated conclusions by leaps and bounds. Allow me to illustrate the expeditious process of eliminating negative thoughts.

Allen engaged in a dispute with his spouse. He created a considerable physical separation between himself and her, proceeded to exit the premises, and forcefully closed the door. Throughout the duration of his stroll in the park, his mind was preoccupied with thoughts of his anger. He was exacerbating the already adverse situation. He was prepared to terminate his marriage. He had grown weary of her persistent complaints. He was visually packing his bags and leaving and hated her. Indeed, she had simply surprised him and broached a subject for which he was ill-prepared. He had experienced a challenging day at the workplace and was not mentally prepared for the level of discourse she anticipated upon his arrival. You exaggerate situations in your mind to such a degree that you envision all potential adverse outcomes. In the instance of Allen, whilst traversing the park, he failed to perceive any positive occurrences. He proceeded amidst the splendid manifestations of the natural world, perceiving naught but darkness and desolation. As he proceeded deeper into his path, he was abruptly cognizant of a juvenile in peril. A young child was on the verge of descending into the canal which meandered alongside the periphery of the park. All of his irate musings came to an abrupt halt, prompting his innate intuition to compel him to embark on a mission to rescue the child. The rationale behind the significance of this explanation lies in the expeditious manner in which we are able to dismiss detrimental thoughts. In that fleeting moment, he momentarily disregarded his disagreement with his spouse and rescued the child.

Think of this. By relinquishing a burdensome thought, you are sparing the inner child from experiencing the immense distress associated with such thoughts. You are permitting yourself to be drawn back into the present moment. Currently, as a means of alleviating stress, an approach known as mindfulness has gained traction, presenting individuals with the opportunity to employ it in order to break free from detrimental thought patterns. When confronted with ambiguity in life or questioning one's own capabilities, it is advisable to inhale through the nostrils and shift focus from the negative thoughts to the act of breathing. Inhale deeply and synchronize your breathing with the count of seven. Exhale slowly and steadily, counting up to ten. You are engaging in the process of regulating the oxygen flow within your body and attaining a state of tranquility. Individuals who exhibit low levels of self-assurance can employ this highly effective strategy to dispel any detrimental thoughts directed at their own personhood. Instead of expressing one's inability to perform a task or perceiving it as excessively challenging, one should engage in deep breathing and release all negative notions. Engage in this practice when you notice self-critical tendencies arise within you, and actively release those critical thoughts, much like Allen managed to do amidst his distractions. Nevertheless, you have the ability to control your own level of distraction. It facilitates the development of self-assurance and empowers you to surmount instances characterized by personal uncertainty.

Consider it from this perspective. Each time you engage in self-deprecating thoughts, you inadvertently contribute to the erosion of self-assurance within yourself. By substituting negativity with a positive action such as focusing on controlled breathing, one prevents their cognitive processes from overpowering them. This exercise is highly beneficial for individuals dealing with stage fright, preparing for interviews, or going through moments of diminished self-assurance.

Try it now. Inhale through the nasal passages for a duration of seven counts, followed by an exhalation of ten counts. Initially, it may pose some difficulty as one tends to be habituated to shallow breathing. As you continue to inhale and exhale, consciously redirect your focus to the present moment. Take notice of all the positive elements in your surroundings. Employ your faculties of olfaction, gustation, tactile perception, auditory perception, and other relevant sensory modalities. To exist in the present moment while relinquishing any detrimental thoughts.

The mental discourse occurring within your mind is merely superfluous noise. With sufficient practice, one can effectively cultivate the capacity to release it, while individuals endowed with confidence possess the aptitude to attenuate internal discourse and focus deeply on the present. Another aspect which proves advantageous in utilizing mindfulness techniques is the cultivation of non-judgmental awareness, wherein one abstains from forming judgments about anything, including oneself. This implies that in the event of an occurrence, culpability is absolved. It is merely an occurrence that transpires. You acquire knowledge from the experience and do not necessitate memorization. One is able to transcend such situations, thus attaining a state of tranquility when engaging with the intricacies of life.

After mastering the exercises outlined in this book, you will notice a remarkable improvement in your levels of confidence and self-restraint. Additionally, one may observe that they tend to draw individuals who exude confidence into their life, thereby replacing those who exploit or undermine their self-assurance. If individuals exploit your kindness, it is advisable to distance yourself from such individuals and seek to surround yourself solely with those who contribute positively to your daily life. Should they choose not to do so, it would be more suitable for you to regard it as their concern rather than yours, as you are presently in the process of bolstering your self-assurance and do not require the presence of individuals who are inclined to undermine it once more.

Introversion, Shyness, And Love

Introversion is primarily a personal attribute shaped by internal emotions, rather than being contingent upon external stimuli. Being an introvert does not inherently lead to a disposition of anxiety and timidity. In contrast, introverts possess a serene demeanor but exhibit remarkable courage similar to that of a lion. They are not easily swayed by external influences as they consistently demonstrate a resolute and astute disposition. Their clarity of purpose leads them to remain steadfast and determined in their pursuit of their goals. To exhibit shyness entails experiencing apprehension towards individuals and the given circumstances. The fact that an individual is unable to deliver an eloquent speech in a social or official setting as a result of shyness should not be regarded as evidence of introversion; rather, it represents a manifestation of fear. Despite their tendency to avoid close proximity with others, introverted individuals do have an inclination to value the presence of those with whom they share an intimate connection.

A considerable number of individuals have erroneously conflated shyness with introversion, leading to an exceedingly startling revelation. Certain individuals with extroverted tendencies desire to enter into matrimony with an individual of a more introverted disposition. Due to their inability to distinguish between introversion and shyness, they find themselves caught in a predicament. The majority of individuals ultimately paired with partners who possessed either an extroverted, introverted, or ambiverted personality trait. These are the aforementioned entities that were previously deliberated to encompass the aforementioned criteria.

Kayla possessed a calm and pleasant demeanor, and her physical appearance was striking. One day, as she sought respite in a shower after the day's toil, she became aware of the piercing screams emanating from her neighboring residence. As it was a hotel room, she possessed the rightful authority to disregard the noise and attend to her own affairs. On each occasion when she needed to handle business matters outside her town, she would make her way to the hotel. This marked one of her journeys, during which she exerted herself throughout the entire day. The utmost significance to her at present was obtaining adequate rest and maintaining a tranquil atmosphere. She had consistently opted for that particular hotel due to its tranquility over an extended duration;

however, on that day, she found herself inclined to question her decision. She simply required a restful slumber, which would have resolved this commotion. Unable to endure the incessant chatter any longer, she departed from her quarters in a state of anger to investigate the source of the disturbance. Upon arriving at the doorstep, she inadvertently overheard the woman angrily exclaiming, "I cannot believe that you would demean me in such a manner." "You demonstrate a complete disregard for the welfare of others, as evidenced by your self-absorption," the tirade persisted. Kayla was compelled to rap on the door. It was inconceivable that she would be able to attain a restful sleep while being left alone in the presence of this woman. The door was ajar, and she proceeded to enter. In light of everything that transpired, Kayla came to the realization that Nora had made an erroneous assessment of Steeve. Upon their initial encounter, she presumed that he was simply exhibiting shyness, oblivious to the fact that Steeve, in reality, identified as an introvert. He preferred solitude. He exhibited introverted tendencies and appeared to lack an enthusiasm for Nora's areas of interest. Nora harbored suspicions that Steeve could potentially be engaging in extramarital activities. In contrast, Steeve, when questioned about his decision to exclude Nora from his life, responded by stating, "I believed she shared similarities with me." In their initial encounter, Steeve erroneously interpreted Nora's reserved demeanor as indicative of introversion. It wasn't long before he discovered that she held completely contrasting views to his own. Nora consistently expressed a desire for engaging in shopping, socializing with friends, and engaging Steeve in meaningful conversation.

Kayla, who shared Steeve's introverted nature, felt compelled to have a candid conversation with Nora, wherein she offered the sagacious counsel that she either devote herself to fostering a meaningful connection with Steeve by embracing his authentic self, or alternatively, consider terminating their relationship and parting ways. After numerous hours, tranquility finally reigned in the surrounding area.

Based on the aforementioned narrative, it becomes evident that a widespread misconception occurs when individuals confuse shyness with introversion. Despite Steeve and Nora successfully cultivating a harmonious living environment through mutual respect for one another's individuality, it is evident that Nora has exerted significant efforts to establish tranquility within her household. When questioned about her handling of the ordeal, she responded by stating, "In order to develop and sustain romantic affection for an introverted individual, one must comprehend the following factors."

1. Don't demand too much.

Introverts do not like it when people ask for too much of them. They have no desire to be perceived as mere placeholders who occupy every vacant spot in your existence. He deeply appreciates his involvement in your life, but wishes to avoid a sense of suffocation resulting from an excessive imposition of your presence.

2. Don't be in haste.

As a result of their reserved disposition, individuals with introverted tendencies tend to prefer a gradual approach when engaging both in physical activities and emotional connections. Expediting the process may provoke his displeasure and prompt his departure.

3. Be original.

Introverted individuals experience deep satisfaction when they encounter individuals who embody originality. He possesses ample intellectual capacity for analysis; thus, there is no need to augment his concerns with a frivolous existence.

4. Love silence

On occasion, individuals who possess introverted qualities may exhibit a preference for abstaining from conversations or eluding interactions initiated by others. His sole desire is to relish in a state of tranquility. Please refrain from attempting to disrupt the ongoing enjoyment. Demonstrate deference to his decision and withdraw by granting him the necessary personal space.

5. Grow listening ears.

Although introverts tend to be reserved, they sometimes have the inclination to engage in conversations. They desire the certainty that an individual possesses sufficient concern to lend them a receptive ear.

6. Be sincere.

Few things bring greater joy to introverts than the genuine sincerity of others. Introverts have a deep comprehension of the challenges associated with finding individuals who can be wholeheartedly relied upon. Individuals who express themselves directly and honestly without using euphemisms or veiled language. Once you have established your credibility and reliability, you can easily persuade them to confide in you at minimal expense.

Comprehensive Instructions For Enhancing Listening Skills

The cultivation of listening abilities constitutes a highly significant tool in the pursuit of emotional intelligence. When discussing emotional intelligence, we are referring to the capacity to comprehend the emotions of others. What could be considered a more valuable token of empathy and comprehension towards others than dedicating oneself to actively and attentively hearing their words? The ability to actively listen provides us with an invaluable means of understanding the lives of others, and possessing such a means carries both a sense of duty and honor. It is imperative to exhibit reverence towards others and refrain from exploiting the authority associated with possessing attentive listening skills. It is imperative that you consistently exercise this authority with integrity and honesty.

An individual possessing adept listening skills has the ability to participate in an entire conversation with minimal verbal contributions or inquiries. They might possess the ability to steer conversations silently through the modification of their non-verbal cues. It is possible that their attention is completely absorbed by the individual speaking, thereby eliminating any inclination to engage in conversation. The extent of variation in individuals' preferences for discussing different topics and the urgency they attach to such discussions may differ depending on their specific needs and circumstances.

The acquisition of effective listening abilities can determine the contrast between being an inadequate communicator and a proficient communicator. An effective communicator possesses the capability to succinctly encapsulate the ideas and perspectives conveyed by the interlocutor. An individual possessing excellent communication skills will excel as a listener due to their ability to actively engage with information, demonstrating strength and meticulous attention to detail. Effective communication relies on the exchange of words between two individuals. In order for robust communication to flourish, it is imperative that a reciprocal feedback loop exists between two entities.

Active listening is the practice of experiencing a specific emotional response towards an individual. Could you recollect a moment in your life when you experienced a profound sense of being supported and cherished? It could potentially be the individual's parent, a schoolteacher, counselor, or any other suitable figure. This exemplifies the exceptional capabilities of an astute listener. They have the capability to instill a sense of intellectual prowess. They are capable of fostering a sense of active participation and meaningful engagement, thereby ensuring equitable and satisfactory interaction. Individuals naturally seek recognition and affirmation, thereby receiving a significant level of validation by simply bestowing attention upon them.

The capacity to accomplish this for individuals is undeniably a crucial aptitude in the realm of art. The majority of therapists acquire the skill of impartial observation, enabling them to effectively detach themselves from the situation at hand. When an individual becomes aware of being heard by others, they experience a sense of their position within society and perceive the potential for profound change that it possesses. Indeed, a significant proportion of individuals who engage in therapeutic treatment for disparate concerns often perceive an imperative necessity for such intervention, oblivious to the fact that their underlying requirements primarily revolve around seeking attentiveness, affection, and the validation of their thoughts and emotions from their counterparts. Individuals may seek therapy without fully comprehending this fact, and over the course of multiple sessions, if the therapist is skilled, they will gradually experience improvement through the process of verbal expression and discussion. Certain individuals have an inherent desire to be heard, yet regrettably, they seldom receive the opportunity to have their voices heard.

Requesting what you require can pose considerable difficulty, hence seeking the assistance of others in lending you an ear can prove beneficial. On certain occasions, it becomes necessary to engage the services of an individual who possesses expertise in order to assist you in your endeavors.

In essence, to cultivate proficiency in listening, one must possess a genuine curiosity for both the world and individuals. It is important to possess a genuine curiosity in understanding the motivations behind people's actions, as well as a penchant for spreading happiness among others. One should aim for a mindset similar to that of a beginner, intrigued by the novelty of every new encounter, as it resembles the curious nature of a child. One ought to appreciate the abundant diversity that exists among individuals and embrace the opportunity to earnestly comprehend those who differ from oneself.

The Rationale For Establishing Objectives

It is essential to acknowledge that when one establishes goals, they fall beyond their sphere of influence. Consequently, excessively fixating on these goals impedes achievement. In contrast, by directing your attention towards your behaviors rather than your objectives, you can effectively accomplish your goals.

You alone possess the capacity to oversee and evaluate your actions. They are elements subject to your control. Therefore, it is imperative to disregard the aspects of your objectives over which you have no control and concentrate solely on the portion within your influence, namely your behaviors. Once you direct your attention towards your actions, consistently and over the course of time, you initiate the process of acquiring all the necessary knowledge to effectively achieve your predetermined objectives.

When one envisions their objective as already accomplished, it places them in a position to concentrate on devising a strategy to bring it to fruition. Behaviors tend to have a short-term duration when we establish objectives; typically, they span a period of seven days. Therefore, one must consider the actions that can be undertaken today, tomorrow, and during the course of this week, document them, and proceed accordingly.

The Definitive Specification of Objectives

It is imperative to exercise prudence, for the present reality is shaped by one's past, by one's previous encounters. If one constrains their future based on their past, they will impede their progress. You must establish ambitious objectives that serve as powerful motivators. Therefore, refrain from halting and inquiring, "What is the method?"

This does not constitute the initial step. The primary stage entails documenting all aspects, and upon doing so, one can successfully forge and mold their own utopia, according to their personal desires and preferences. It commences with a straightforward procedure of capturing these generalized dream impulses and subsequently delineating them with greater precision.

That exemplifies the efficacy of setting goals. There exists a realm beyond a mere comprehension of transcribing thoughts onto paper. Something happens. One becomes a creator when they establish objectives and document them in writing. You gain a distinct perspicacity while simultaneously possessing the ability to actualize them.

Hence, it is imperative to ensure that you not only establish objectives but also gain absolute clarity on the underlying motivations driving your pursuit of these goals. It is an established truth that goal-setting possesses a fundamental essence capable of transforming one's life. The key lies in the fact that purpose holds more potency than the ultimate result.

The rationale for establishing objectives." or "The underlying purpose of setting goals.

The significance of this concept lies in the fact that the essence of goals is not merely the attainment of material possessions, but rather the transformative impact they have on one's character and personal development. I am presently in the process of acknowledging this fact. The majority of individuals establish goals without adequate foresight. They possess a strong inclination and direct their attention towards material possessions. There is no issue with that; I encourage you to pursue as many endeavors as you desire, as it is an integral aspect of life.

It is an integral aspect of the manifestation process in achieving desired outcomes through goal-setting. If one's sole preoccupation is merely acquiring possessions, it could potentially compromise the fundamental essence of one's character and undermine their ambition to manifest their desired outcomes in life. It is essential to exercise caution.

While the allure of financial gains can provide limited motivation, cultivating the ability to materialize prosperity both economically and physically not only offers greater fulfillment, but also positively impacts both oneself and those in their proximity. Possessing the liberty afforded by financial resources or being empowered to extend support to others through the practice of paying it forward typically serves as a greater source of motivation than any other factor.

Enhancing Self-Perception

Strategy 2

The initial approach described in this segment entails assuming responsibility for one's own well-being. Upon awakening each morning, I implore you to welcome yourself in front of the mirror with a gracious smile. In the event that you are unable to conceive of any favorable thoughts, it is advisable to take a moment to pause and engage in the process of mental imagery. The concept you are attempting to envision pertains to a specific point in your life characterized by a profound sense of joy. It can occur at any point within the timeframe of your life, and I request that you employ this imagery whenever you experience pessimistic sentiments towards any matter during the upcoming week. Rather than permitting negative thoughts to linger, it is advisable to envision a state of contentment and refrain from dwelling on unfavorable occurrences.

Gaze upon your reflection in the mirror, contemplate a positive thought, and subsequently make proper arrangements for the day ahead. Take care of yourself. Ensure that you appear presentable and devote attention to your appearance by inspecting yourself in a full-length mirror prior to departing your residence. Utilize footwear that provides comfort, as it facilitates enhanced stability and steadiness. Please ensure you attire yourself in garments that offer a comfortable fit, appropriate for the activities you have planned for the day. Approach the world with a cheerful countenance – encompassing even those individuals you encounter who typically evoke feelings of self-doubt within you. Acquiring proficiency will require a significant investment of time; however, the cultivation of positivity is instrumental in enhancing the quality of your life. Should this emanate from within you, the subsequent outcomes will indeed be exceedingly favorable.

It is imperative that you take care of yourself as it is your duty. It is imperative that you consume appropriate dietary choices. It is imperative to ensure that you obtain an appropriate duration of sleep. These notions are generally understood, yet have you considered the extent to which you cultivate optimism and self-empowerment within yourself? It is highly probable that you underestimate your accomplishments in life, which is a significant error. It is imperative that you overcome the notion that you lack value in dedicating time to self-care, and recognize that prioritizing oneself is of paramount importance in one's life. YOU won't gain confidence and self-esteem while you put others ahead of yourself.

Third strategic approach – Embracing volunteer engagement

You might not be accustomed to engaging in volunteer work, but genuine volunteering does not revolve around providing assistance solely to seek validation from others. It pertains to extending assistance without any ulterior motives or expectations of reciprocity. This exemplifies genuine volunteerism, which contributes to a sense of self-fulfillment as it is driven by pure intentions devoid of any ulterior motives. You are not actively pursuing affirmation or approval. You are merely engaging in this action out of your inherent kindness. Whether that entails partaking in the act of baking a cake for a neighbor who resides in solitude or extending an offer to accompany a friend's canine companion for a leisurely stroll, opt to volunteer your assistance on a regular basis. Engaging with a nearby animal shelter that is in need of assistance is an excellent initial step, as animals do not possess the capacity to provide approval. What they will provide you with is a sense of accomplishment that requires no external validation. Likewise, it is possible to pay a visit to patients in a medical facility who lack company, offer voluntary services at a hospital boutique, assist in activities at your nearby church, or alternatively, contribute by serving meals at a community-based soup kitchen. You possess the awareness that your actions are driven by righteous intentions, and you require no validation from others. Nevertheless, by engaging in these actions, you are reinforcing your worth as an individual.

The efficacy of volunteerism stems from the fact that it encompasses more than mere acts of giving. The essence lies in the act of bestowing without any anticipation of recognition or acknowledgement whatsoever. When considering the scenario wherein a parent persistently underscores a child's failure to meet parental expectations, the resultant effect is the development of a pervasive sense of inadequacy in the child as they mature. Nevertheless, upon closer scrutiny of this circumstance, it becomes evident that the parent's considerable contributions to the child were not wholeheartedly given, but rather came with certain conditions attached. Whenever you engage in such actions, you invariably find yourself dissatisfied with the outcomes. In the realm of volunteering, you contribute selflessly without any attached obligations. It is possible that someone may express gratitude, though it is also possible that they may not do so. When engaging in volunteer work, the focus is not on the outcomes. It pertains to offering selflessly without any anticipation of reciprocity. Once you acquire the capacity to accomplish that, a rapid transformation in your being shall ensue. You commence expressing gratitude towards your identity. You develop an enhanced sense of self-worth and cultivate self-esteem, which should be the underlying purpose of engaging in volunteer work. You refrain from boasting or anticipating gratitude, as you are content with receiving modest expressions of appreciation. You have the opportunity to experience a sense of fulfillment, making you feel that you have accomplished something of value, and it is as uncomplicated as that.

Individuals who experience self-esteem issues frequently seek validation from others. They possess uncertainty regarding their stability in life. Volunteerism, to a certain extent, provides a different vantage point on this matter. The canine you accompanied on a stroll earlier may not have expressed gratitude; nevertheless, partaking in this activity likely brought you pleasure, all while supporting a philanthropic organization in fulfilling their crucial mission. Assistance provided to a child in completing their homework stems from a desire to nurture their educational growth and promote the acquisition of learning abilities. One should engage in this activity not driven by personal expectations, but rather by the understanding that it will be of value to the child.

Engaging in voluntary work also cultivates a sense of intrinsic worth and significance in one's life, particularly for individuals grappling with self-esteem challenges who may tend to overlook this aspect of their existence and turn inward. I regret to inform you that you will be unable to allocate time for such activities due to your voluntary commitments. Please proceed to prepare a cake for your neighboring household. Rectify their garden gate solely on account of your desire. If they inquire about the amount they owe you, kindly offer a sincere smile and convey, "It is my sincere delight to render this service without expecting anything in return."

How can family members and close friends provide assistance in this situation?

When acquaintances exhibiting low self-esteem come to your attention, there are several pivotal measures you can undertake.

Show them that you genuinely value their well-being and reassure them of your commitment to support and protect them. One can showcase their emotions by displaying gentleness, actively engaging in attentive listening, or devoting quality time to their presence.

Assist in recalling the positive aspects – while one cannot completely alter individuals' negative perception of themselves, it is possible to challenge this by aiding them in recollecting noteworthy accomplishments, such as their remarkable achievements or positive contributions.

Refrain from attributing blame to others - individuals with diminished self-esteem often assign responsibility for negative experiences, including mental health concerns, to themselves. Assure them that this is not their mistake and refrain from instructing them to 'compose yourself.'

Please endeavor to maintain a steadfast approach, as low self-esteem is typically cultivated over an extended period of time. Altering an individual's perception of their own capabilities can be a time-consuming process, often requiring regular reassurance and support.

Communicate to them that periodic feelings of distress are natural, as nobody experiences constant contentment and determination, and emphasize the importance of not feeling obligated to fulfill unreasonable aspirations.

Exhibit supportiveness – when your companion or relative engages in a self-improvement endeavor or seeks guidance from a counselor, it is essential to display a supportive and positive attitude. You may also extend your kind assistance by offering generous support, such as providing childcare services to facilitate their attendance at meetings.

Assist in facilitating the search for appropriate treatment – if there are concerns that low self-esteem is contributing to a mental health issue, encourage and support your companion or relative in pursuing suitable treatment.

Self-improvement resources

Please take into consideration these key guidelines in order to enhance your self-esteem.

• Engage in physical activities that you find enjoyable.

• Allocate your time to engage with individuals who possess constructive and stable traits.

• Demonstrate a willingness to assist and accommodate others.

• Endeavor to avoid drawing comparisons between oneself and others.

• Endeavor to engage in regular physical activities, maintain a nutritious diet, and ensure sufficient rest.

- Be firm in your decisions – do not allow individuals to be treated without proper respect.

- Employ self-improvement resources and online platforms to develop a solid foundation of knowledge and skills, such as assertiveness training or mindfulness techniques.

- Acquire the ability to question your unfavorable beliefs.

- Recognize and affirm your positive attributes and areas of expertise.

- Develop the practice of recalling and verbally expressing constructive statements about oneself.

Why is Self-Esteem of utmost importance?

Self-worth refers to individuals' perceptions regarding their inherent value and personal significance. It is also connected to the range of emotions individuals undergo, which can differ in terms of their sense of significance or indignity. Self-respect is integral as it significantly impacts individuals' decisions and choices. Self-esteem plays a crucial role in instilling inspiration as it greatly enhances the probability that individuals will attend to their own needs and seek to fulfill their true potential. Individuals who possess elevated self-esteem exhibit a stronger commitment to self-care and a dedicated pursuit of personal aspirations and goals. Individuals who possess diminished self-esteem tend to perceive themselves as undeserving of positive outcomes or capable of achieving them, resulting in a tendency to neglect crucial matters and exhibit reduced resilience and adaptability in the face of adversity. Individuals with higher self-esteem may possess distinct goals, whereas those with lower self-esteem typically exhibit reduced motivation to actively pursue them until they are successfully achieved.

Self-esteem, to a certain extent, can be viewed as an abstract concept that is challenging for individuals lacking it to fully comprehend and appreciate its significance in terms of personal experience. An effective method for individuals experiencing lower self-esteem to cultivate an understanding of higher self-esteem is to reflect upon their personal values and assess their sentiments towards various aspects of their lives. As an illustration, a considerable number of individuals indeed hold a preference for automobiles. Given that automobiles hold great importance to these individuals, they accord substantial attention to the maintenance of their vehicles. They exercise sound discernment concerning the choice of parking locations, the frequency of vehicle maintenance, and their driving behaviors. They have the possibility to modify the vehicle and subsequently display it to others with a sense of satisfaction. Self-esteem pertains to the appreciation, nurturing, and contentment one derives from the self. When children embrace themselves, they become consequential and precious to society, exhibiting utmost care and regard for their own well-being. They exercise discernment regarding their own abilities, thereby enhancing their value rather than diminishing it.

Recognize And Address Concerns Regarding Your Self-Esteem

A multitude of problems can emanate from low self-esteem. With which ones do you encounter difficulties, and what are the reasons for these challenges? What steps can be taken to address these concerns and enhance the quality of your current lifestyle? This marks the initial phase of our comprehensive seven-step program aimed at immediately enhancing your self-esteem.

Step 1: Confronting the Challenges Arising from Low Self-Esteem

Relationship Issues

For individuals who possess strong self-assurance and have achieved a sense of inner contentment, long-term partnerships or matrimony provide a fertile ground to discover affection, validation, and during challenges, unwavering assistance. Individuals who possess a diminished sense of self-worth tend to experience significant adverse effects on their relationships due to such emotional states.

Researchers are discovering that self-esteem not only influences individuals' self-perception, but also exerts a detrimental effect on their anticipations pertaining to partners and relationships. It necessitates reliance on your partner for all validation and recognition. Your personal lack of confidence renders a relationship incapable of offering the essential qualities that a healthy relationship encompasses.

In times of adversity, individuals with diminished self-esteem anticipate a lack of assistance from their significant others rather than expecting their support. They anticipate their partner's disapproval and fear a loss of affection.

Jealousy

The association between the relationship problems we have just discussed and feelings of jealousy and low self-esteem is significant. It is plausible to surmount feelings of jealousy and enhance one's sense of self-worth, however, this endeavor necessitates a considerable investment of time. It takes reflection. It requires diligent effort, but it is achievable.

The perilous nature of jealousy arising from inadequate self-confidence stems from empirical evidence suggesting that the confluence of these sentiments can elicit neurological responses akin to the shock or grieving process triggered by the loss of a cherished individual. The powerful negative effect arises from the simultaneous presence of envy and a diminished sense of self-worth.

Due to your diminished sense of self-worth, you may hold the belief that your partner maintains an unwavering openness to other individuals, as you perceive yourself to be undeserving of love. These emotions render you susceptible to the onset of bitter envy at any given moment. Overcoming jealousy requires significant support and personal determination, but it is a surmountable challenge.

Depression/Anxiety/Panic Attacks

This represents the utmost peril among the various manifestations of low self-esteem that one may encounter. Depression, anxiety, and panic attacks are three significant psychological conditions that can result in severe implications for both one's self-esteem and overall mental well-being.

Depression

There exists a robust correlation between depression and self-esteem regarding the shared experience of feelings of inadequacy. Subsequently, when lowered self-esteem precipitates depression, it ensues a twofold impact. This cognitive process is commonly induced by depression, while diminished self-worth can elicit similar effects.

An individual exhibiting diminished self-confidence may easily succumb to the tripartite formation of adverse cognitions, encompassing a sense of personal insignificance, skepticism towards the trustworthiness and acceptance of others, and a pessimistic outlook on forthcoming events.

Anxiety and Panic Attacks

The relationship between anxiety and panic disorders is more nuanced than that of depression, yet it can yield equally detrimental effects. Low self-esteem gives rise to uncertainty in all decision-making endeavors, leading to the potential development of anxiety and panic episodes. As a result of lacking self-confidence and harboring feelings of inadequacy and incompetence, individuals with low self-esteem often lack the ability to make sound decisions.

Furthermore, the experience of anxiety and panic has the potential to culminate in the development of phobias, thereby further constricting the scope of one's life activities. An individual who possesses diminished self-confidence will lack the necessary assurance to surmount such challenges. They will hold the belief that accomplishing such a task is unattainable.

Action Plan

Low self-esteem can give rise to a plethora of challenges in relationships, such as envy, melancholy, distress, and episodes of apprehension and panic. Diligent effort on your part can effectively address the sentiments of inferiority and self-doubt that individuals with low self-esteem often encounter.

- In the circumstance that you are engaged in a romantic partnership, it is advised that you consistently document at least one admirable attribute of your own contribution within said relationship on a daily basis. Regardless of the events that transpire within a given day, ensure to consistently undertake this singular task on a daily basis.

• Now, apply the same principle to your own individuality, separate from the context of your relationship. Dedicate a few minutes twice a day to express gratitude towards yourself for a quality or accomplishment you possess. Write this down.

• In fact, a majority of individuals tend to encounter more instances of acceptance rather than rejection, regardless of their personal perceptions. Make a concerted effort to observe regularly whether the individuals in your social circle exhibit kindness or display a tendency to dismiss or disregard you. The most effective strategy to address diminished self-esteem is to regularly expose oneself to daily, incessant experiences of acceptance rather than rejection in order to attain personal growth and develop a realistic self-perception.

• Maintain a record of all these encounters in a journal, and upon the conclusion of each week, convene with the individual you hold utmost trust in and reflect upon these incidents. Did you actually receive affirmation or did you encounter rejection?

• Establishing a constructive relationship provides you with a favorable frame of reference in your existence. To cultivate a healthier self-relationship, it is advisable to strategically place affirmative messages in prominent locations throughout your residence to ensure daily exposure.

Negatives Thoughts

Negativity persists and shows no signs of abating in the foreseeable future. It is a permanent fixture, impervious to any potential actions that may seek to hinder its permanence. It will restrain you, impede your progress, and greatly diminish the quality of life. It is essential to have the readiness and capability to contemplate the potential existence of negativity in your life, and the initial step towards achieving this is to ascertain if you possess negative traits or tendencies.

Should you uncover the fact that you possess negative qualities, please refrain from experiencing despondency. Should you find yourself in such a situation, there is absolutely no justification for maintaining a pessimistic outlook over an extended period of time. There is no need for concern regarding obstacles impeding your progress or restricting your growth; you have the ability to acquire the knowledge and techniques to effectively overcome and eliminate them. One can explore the methods by which one can effectively overcome those pessimistic thoughts, thereby cultivating a more optimistic mindset and harnessing the full potential of positive thinking.

Inevitably, it is not uncommon to discover certain unfavorable characteristics or pessimistic thoughts within oneself - a natural aspect of being human. Nonetheless, it is important to bear in mind that there exists a possibility for cultivating a positive mindset, should one choose to do so. Optimism holds significant importance, and it is within your power to cultivate it. One can acquire the skills necessary to regulate their thought patterns, enabling them to transform their entire cognitive framework from pessimistic to optimistic.

What is Negative Thinking?

Negative thinking encompasses all types of thoughts that possess an inherent pessimistic or adverse nature. Negativity is seldom conducive to productivity, as it directs attention towards identifying problems rather than exploring potential solutions. Consequently, negative thinking can readily intensify and perpetuate itself. When one's focus is fixated on dwelling upon past actions and regrets rather than embracing the possibilities of the present, productivity and effectiveness become hindered. This type of mindset is generally encouraged to be avoided due to its lack of productivity. Merely refraining from a certain action does not imply an understanding or recognition of the appropriate course of action. You are merely eliminating one of the myriad possibilities from your catalogue.

Negative thinking can manifest as an exclusively negative mindset, wherein thoughts revolve around self-blame or perceiving the day as exceptionally unpleasant, leading to an overall negative connotation. Additionally, it may manifest as a complete lack of precision, for example, in the form of a cognitive distortion. Indeed, subsequently, you will be provided with a comprehensive compilation of various cognitive distortions commonly encountered, aiming to cultivate the ability to discern negative thoughts from the outset.

By harboring these negative thoughts, you are affording negativity the authority to dictate the course of your life. Once more, reflect upon the sequence you have observed thus far, which serves as the bedrock of the comprehensive approach known as cognitive-behavioral therapy (CBT). The propagation of negativity occurs when it is introduced into any given situation. Negative emotions are pernicious and easily spreadable; even aspects of oneself previously untouched by negativity will swiftly become entangled in it if it is permitted to flourish and taint adjoining thoughts and emotions.

It is possible that you have been exposed to information regarding negative thinking, yet it is likely that you disregarded it due to a perceived lack of relevance to your personal circumstances. However, at some point, you awaken to the realization that your existence lacks purpose and excitement, and that the possibility of pessimistic thoughts, which seemed distant previously, is actually not as remote as initially perceived. You diligently acquire knowledge through extensive reading and immerse yourself in various forms of media pertaining to the subject matter. Additionally, you make attempts to implement certain expedient remedies you come across; however, none of these approaches prove to be effective. You desire an approach that is grounded in practicality.

Begin by conducting a sincere evaluation of your pessimism. Presented below is an inventory detailing the prevailing components of negative thought patterns. Should any or all of the aforementioned items align with your interests, please continue perusing the following content. You possess a pessimistic outlook. This literary work will facilitate your comprehension of the origins of negative thought patterns, as well as the factors that consistently prompt and perpetuate them. And it will outline techniques for consciously modifying one's thought patterns in order to align with an objective perspective on reality, thereby fostering a state of equilibrium, positivity, and productivity in one's life. Please allocate a sufficient amount of time to carefully review the list provided below and, if desired, supplement it with additional items.

"You exhibit tendencies of a pessimistic mindset if:

You exhibit an excessive inclination towards criticism and judgement, exhibiting an unwavering belief in the correctness of your perspective. Consequently, individuals find it arduous to maintain proximity with you.

You possess a general sense of cynicism towards life and your thoughts are often preoccupied and hindered by pessimistic considerations of potential negative outcomes.

One's potential in life cannot be realized due to a lack of trust or belief in one's ability to take advantage of the abundant opportunities that exist.

You are displaying escalating levels of anger, morbidity, and moodiness, experiencing a pervasive lack of enjoyment in all aspects of life.

Your pessimistic outlook towards individuals and occurrences is primarily rooted in an intuitive perception that has been refined over an extended span of time.

Upon introspection, you have conducted a thorough self-evaluation and acknowledged aspects of your life that are dissatisfactory, as they induce a sense of disempowerment and imposed limitations.

Differentiating Emotions

A notable disparity arises among emotions, feelings, moods, and affection, all of which manifest within the same subgroup within the realm of affective neuroscience.

Sensation: Not all sensations encountered by an individual necessarily convey an emotional response. In terms of emotions, a sensation is regarded as a distinct event signifying an emotion exclusively experienced by the individual undergoing the emotional state.

Moods: These encompass one's affective and subjective state. An individual has the option to express either positive or negative affective states. The sensation may be influenced by insufficient sleep, inadequate nourishment, facial demeanor, and consumption of alcohol. Attitudes generally exhibit less intensity compared to emotions and typically lack a corresponding stimulus.

Affection: This term is commonly employed to depict the subjective encounter of an emotion or sentiment. In the field of psychology, this concept is employed to elucidate the manner in which an individual engages with a stimulus within their surroundings.

The Significance and Worth of Emotions

Emotions exert a substantial influence on our cognitive processes and behavioral responses. Emotions play an integral role in our daily lives, providing us with the impetus to take action and make informed decisions that shape the trajectory of our existence. The subsequent examples delineate the fundamental functions that emotions fulfill:

Rationale: Various emotional states encountered by an individual serve as catalysts for their proactive behavior. As an illustration, anger can be described as an emotional response that arises when a particular circumstance does not align with one's preferences. Consequently, individuals are motivated to take action and modify the situation in order to alleviate their anger. Fear is a sentiment that additionally aids an individual in responding by either seeking refuge or taking measures to retaliate. In such instances, emotions assume a considerable role in facilitating an individual's actions, thereby instigating certain physiological alterations as a result of situational stimuli.

Statement: Emotions are recognized as having a crucial impact, as they furnish individuals with essential information required to effectively modify a situation in alignment with their specific preferences. As an example, in situations where an individual experiences feelings of guilt, it is probable that they will contemplate the reality that their actions have diverged from the established societal norms, ethical guidelines, and personal values.

Therefore, emotions can be characterized as a means of interpersonal transmission, through which the brain receives and processes emotional data, influencing sensory responses and rational behavior. As an illustration, in the event that an individual encounters an armed individual, the sensation of fear will serve as a prompt that advises them to retreat.

Interpersonal communication: The significance of emotions in the process of engaging with others cannot be disregarded. This is due to their capacity to facilitate efficient communication among individuals. The external appearances individuals exhibit aid others in comprehending the emotions they are undergoing. In this manner, individuals will acquire the knowledge necessary to manage such situations without causing any offense. When an individual is in a state of tears, for instance, the counterpart will readily discern the underlying emotion of sadness, thereby devising means of solace that extend beyond light-hearted banter pertaining to a specific circumstance.

The impact of emotions on thoughts: Typically, there exists a substantial alignment between an individual's cognitive processes, recollections, and the affective states they encounter. The recollections of individuals generally encompass the range of emotions experienced during the unfolding of specific events. Consequently, emotions can be deemed to fulfill essential functions in the recollection of factual information. For example, individuals frequently experience greater ease in retrieving positive memories when they are in a state of happiness, and conversely, they tend to access negative memories more readily in moments of anger. The values, beliefs, and attitudes individuals typically uphold are often contingent upon their emotional state. They possess the ability to shape the cognitive processes of an individual, with the potential for both positive and negative impact. It is imperative, henceforth, for an individual to be mindful of their emotions, ensuring that they engage in critical thinking devoid of biases.

Emotions serve as indicators of the dynamics and nature of the interpersonal relationship being forged. Individuals engaging in social interaction can discern the essence of that interaction by evaluating the emotions and attitudes conveyed. An example of this can be observed in the context of a marital relationship, where it becomes readily apparent to discern feelings of dissatisfaction and repulsion through the outward expressions of one partner.

Emotional expressions also serve as a conduit for the manifestation of socially desirable behavior. Social interaction is often conveyed through the facial expressions displayed by an individual. In this particular scenario, a distinct countenance can serve as an indication for individuals to conduct themselves in a desirable manner or in accordance with particular societal norms and principles. For example, when an adolescent enters a room in which adults are engaged in a grave deliberation, the mother may adopt a countenance of displeasure, consequently prompting the teenager to promptly vacate the premises. Facial gestures encompass a wide range of emotions, including anger, happiness, sorrow, curiosity, and apprehension. The information conveyed by these utterances facilitates appropriate action by an individual.

Emotions are also regarded as highly important in the realm of social and cultural functions. This is due to their role in facilitating coordination and organization within a culture. Members of the community have the capacity to resolve intricacies within the societal framework, thereby facilitating the attainment and sustenance of harmony and stability. In this manner, a community can coexist harmoniously and effectively mitigate any potential disharmony. Certain cultural norms regarding emotional expression assist individuals in comprehending and regulating their emotions, thereby mitigating potential harm. Individuals are instructed in the process of modifying their emotions whenever they encounter them. In numerous cultures, these societal norms pertaining to emotions are acquired during the formative years.

In this context, it can be comprehended that emotions consistently serve as a compass, influencing and directing various aspects of an individual's life. This phenomenon arises due to their persistent influence on our behavior and cognitive processes. It is imperative that we consistently delve into our emotional landscape in order to gain insight into their influence on our identity formation and their role in fostering healthy connections, as emotions serve as a means for self-discovery and as a reflection of the impact of past experiences on our personal journeys. The majority of an individual's actions are influenced by emotions, hence it is crucial to comprehend the underlying causes and develop strategies to effectively manage those specific feelings.

Primary emotions can be described as the initial and immediate emotional reactions we exhibit in response to a particular stimulus. They are usually followed by secondary emotions which appear to be more defended. People possess a great deal of awareness when it comes to secondary emotions, such as anger, which commonly arise as a defense mechanism to shield oneself from feelings of hurt or fear that may be overwhelming their sense of anxiety. People must have a thorough comprehension of primary emotions in order to recognize the sense of vulnerability they encounter prior to expressing an emotion.

Primary emotions can demonstrate either advantageous or disadvantageous characteristics. Maladaptive emotions refer to the emotional states we currently experience as a result of our past experiences. For example, if a person is referred to as unintelligent during their early childhood, it is possible that they may experience feelings of shame or profound emotional distress in their later years as adults.

In general, maladaptive emotions are not indicative of one's true character; rather, they are simply emotions. By effectively modifying maladaptive emotions, individuals can foster their transformation into adaptive ones, thereby empowering them to attain their life aspirations.

What Factors Contribute To The Erosion Of Our Self-Confidence?

If self-assurance holds such paramount importance, why do a significant number of individuals encounter challenges in attaining it? This question implies that there was a specific period in your life during which you possessed an ample amount of self-assurance. Do you remember when? If you are unable to do so, perhaps contemplate the remarkable valor exhibited by young children. Consider the persistence displayed by young children as they persistently endeavor to rise to their feet, even if their posterior may still be sore from a recent tumble. They move with unsteady strides across the room, repeatedly succumbing to falls that reopen their recently healed knee injuries. With the passage of time, they now find themselves in the process of maturing and engage in the recitation of poetry within the confines of teeming school auditoriums. Occasionally faltering on the lines, they gather their composure and resume, ultimately concluding to a thunderous applause. Furthermore, they actively participate in academic discourse, eagerly volunteering their raised hands to provide answers, eloquently expressing their thoughts and sentiments with unwavering self-assurance.

Observe the identical individual, now in their adolescent years: eliciting a greeting from them towards visitors proves to be a challenging endeavor; only those who possess absolute certainty in their response and possess the desire to engage raise their hands. Furthermore, they refrain from engaging in any form of public speech, regardless of the magnitude of the audience.

Now consider the mature individual who would prefer to abstain from eating rather than venture into an unfamiliar dining establishment, or consistently opts to occupy a seat positioned towards the rear of the lecture hall, the place of worship, the venue, and so forth.

So, may I inquire about the events that transpired between the intervening period? In addition to the reservation imposed by natural limitations and inherent mindfulness of oneself and others, certain individuals experience a diminishment of this inherent confidence as a result of deficiencies in their upbringing and social interactions. Some deficiencies encompass the continual provision of criticism, leading to a diminished sense of capability, strength, or intelligence. Insufficient support from individuals of importance can lead to a sense of your endeavors or accomplishments being deemed insignificant, disregarded or you being seen as unimportant to others.

Being subjected to comparisons with others, even when done with the misguided intention of desiring me to achieve a similar level of excellence as yourself, severely undermines my confidence. When my perceived weaknesses are juxtaposed with your strengths, it leads to the devaluation of my capacities, skills, value, and undermines my self-assurance.

Furthermore, we have previously discussed the issue surrounding unreasonably elevated expectations imposed by both parental figures and societal pressures.

These are merely a limited selection of prevalent instances that have the ability to gradually diminish one's self-assurance. Indeed, there is a positive development you should be aware of: it is possible for you to regain the confidence that was once lost and maintain it indefinitely. Could you please explain the process you use to accomplish that? Acquire this knowledge in the following segments.

www.ingramcontent.com/pod-product-compliance
Lightning Source LLC
Chambersburg PA
CBHW070304120526
44590CB00017B/2556